The Illustrative Anthology of
Pirate Jokes

By
Teddy Stoecklein

Portland, Maine

Published by Cowboy Yoyo, LLC
PO Box 4264
Portland, ME 04107

© 2019 by Teddy Stoecklein

ISBN: 978-0-578-22804-4

Printed in the United States of America
First Edition
First Printing

Illustrations by Teddy Stoecklein
Cover by Lulu Stoecklein

To my little bucs, Lulu and Wylie.

How to Tell a Pirate Joke

I have traveled the high seas and heard a lot of tall tales, but pirate jokes have always had a special place in my heart. Over the years, I've collected many, even written a few, to create what I consider to be the 50 best pirate jokes. The next time you're marooned on a beach, warming your toes by a campfire, give these pirate jokes a go.

Before you begin, it's important to know that pirate jokes are not easy to deliver. Most often, they come in two stages, the setup and the punchline. The setup is best delivered in your everyday voice, but the punchline **must** be delivered with a thick, pirate accent, the thicker the better. To help with your delivery, you'll find these punchlines written phonetically in bold.

There are probably over a thousand pirate jokes that use the sound "aaargh!" They're easy and fun to think of. While seemingly endless, I've curated this collection to include only my favorites.

Why are pirates called pirates?

'Cause they ARRRGH!!!

What do you call an anxious pirate in a crowded harbor?

A nervous wreck.

What kind of grades did the pirate get in school?

High seas.

Why do pirates love Black Friday?

The sales.

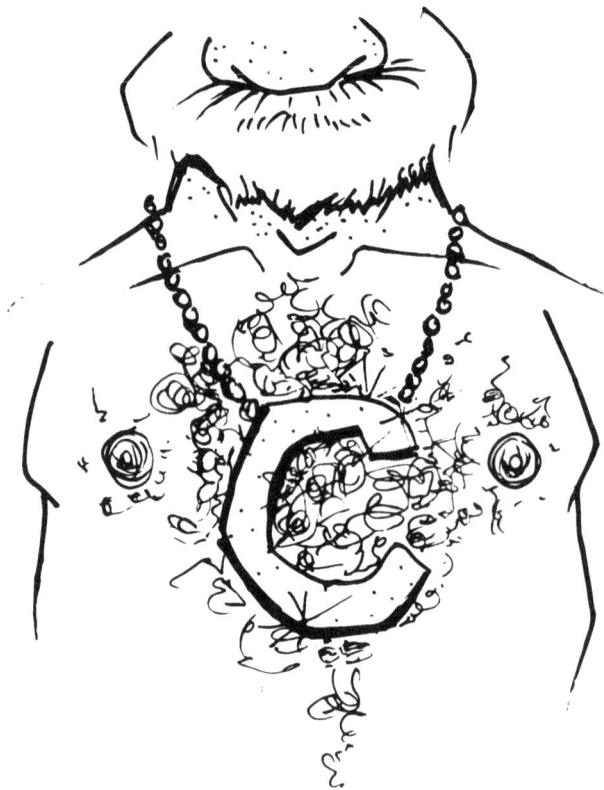

What's a pirate's favorite letter in the alphabet?

Most people will say the "aaargh," to which the answer is a sharp ...

No! The SEA!

A pirate went to the dermatologist and said, **"Aye, Doc, I've got some moles on me back. Can ya give em a look?"**

The doc checked them out and said not to worry. "They're benign."

The pirate responded, **"Count again. I think thar be ten."**

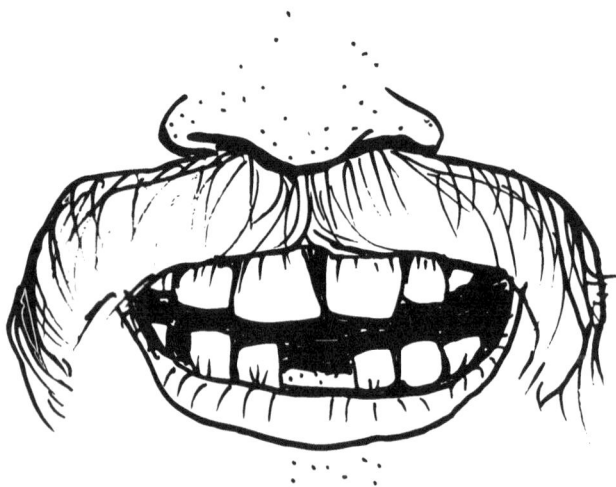

What did the pirate ask the lumberjack while looking for a toothpick?

Can ya sliver me some timbers?

What did the pirate give to wrestle a crocodile?

An arm and a leg.

What do you call a pirate drinking coffee with a doughnut?

A dunkin' sailor.

Why couldn't anyone play cards on the pirate ship?

Because the captain was standing on the deck.

How much did the pirate pay to have his ears pierced?

A buc-an-ear.

Why did the pirate cover his gold with blueberries?

He wanted to berry his treasure.

What's orange and sounds like a parrot?

A carrot.

Whom does the pirate hire
to build his ship?

An arrrghitect.

What's a pirate's favorite kind of movie?

Anything rated arrrgh!

Whom does a pirate root for during the World Cup?

Arrrgentina.

What's a pirate's favorite day at the gym?

Arrrms and legs.

What's a pirate's favorite ab workout?

Da plank.

What did the pirate say
on his 80th birthday?

Aye, matey.

Who cleans the captain's cabin?

A mermaid.

What's a pirate's favorite fish?

The swordfish.

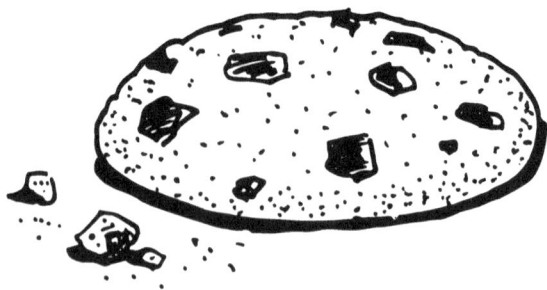

What's a pirate's favorite cookie?

Chips Ahoy!

Where do pirates get their meats?

Arrrby's.

How did the pirate lose his hand?

First fight with a shark.

How did he lose his eye?

First day with a hook.

What does a pirate use to till the soil in his garden?

A land ho!

What do you call a pirate who works at Starbucks?

A barrrista.

Where does a pirate get his
beard trimmed?

The barrrber shop.

Why do pirate's like Golden Corral?

The salad barrrgh.

FOR A GOOD
TIME SEND
LETTER TO
~

Where does a pirate go to the bathroom.

The poop deck.

Where does a pirate go when he's sick?

The docks.

Where does a pirate get gas?

A shell station.

Who is a pirate's favorite author?

J. Arrrgh Arrrgh Tolkien.

What is a pirate's favorite dance?

The Charrr ... leston.

Why did the pirate have trouble tying knots?

Arrrthritis.

How does a pirate get termites off his ship?

He gets an arrrdvark.

What's a pirate's favorite holiday?

Arrrbor Day.

Where does a pirate keep his cash?

The sandbank.

What does a pirate drink on Halloween?

Boo-tea.

Why did the pirate lose the spelling bee?

He was missing an *i*.

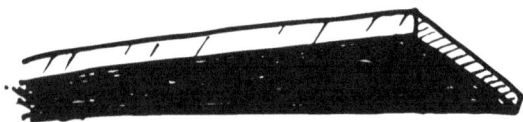

Why don't pirates shower before they walk the plank?

Because they usually wash up onshore.

Who is a pirate's favorite golfer?

Arrrnold Palmer.

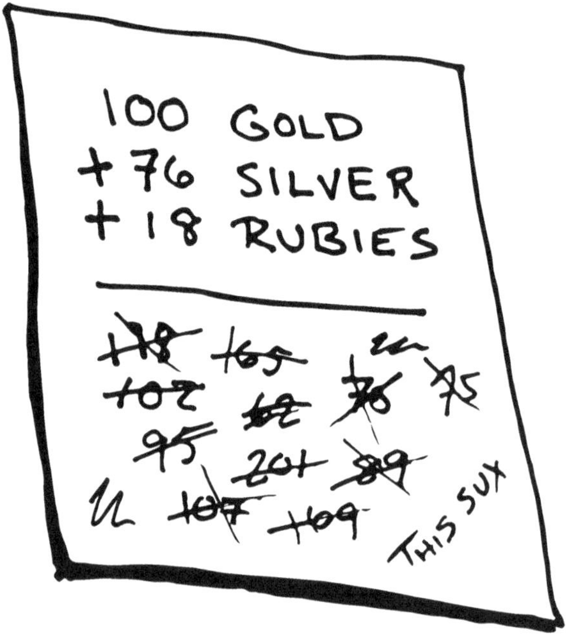
100 GOLD
+76 SILVER
+18 RUBIES
THIS SUX

What is a pirate's worst subject?

Arrrithmetic.

How does a pirate find buried treasure?

He hires an arrrchaeologist.

What's a pirate's favorite dive?

The cannonball.

CAPTAIN

Where does a pirate get his portrait painted?

An arrrt studio.

What happened to Captain Bluebeard when he fell into the Red Sea?

He was marooned.

At a pub, a young lady asked a pirate if he knew where the restroom was.

He pointed to a door in the back and said, **"Thar she blows."**

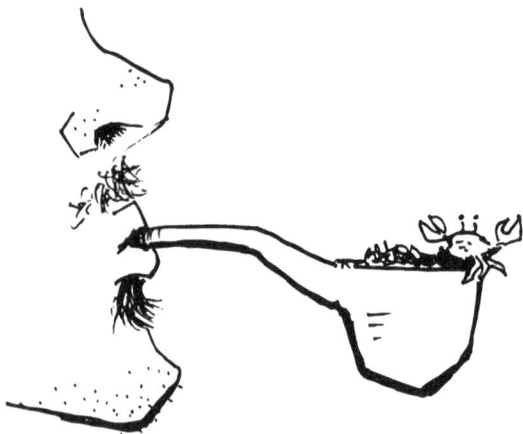

What does a pirate pack in his pipe?

Seaweed.

Who is the greatest pirate of all time?

Roberto Clemente.

Roberto Clemente won two World Series and 12 Gold Glove Awards with the Pittsburgh Pirates (1960-1972). He was also awarded the Presidential Medal of Freedom. Other acceptable answers are Bill Mazeroski and Willie Stargell.

The Ghost of Captain Mac

In the early 1800s, a notorious pirate haunted the North Atlantic islands, from Nova Scotia to the Outer Banks. His name was Captain Mac, for his mother was a Micmac Indian from the Gulf of Maine. Coincidentally, his father was Scotch-Irish.

Captain Mac was a gifted sailor, thief and boxer. He was gregarious, always drawing a crowd, but come evening's end, he'd disappear into the night, leaving people with empty pockets and change purses. If a pub had a safe, it'd surely be looted. In most cases, he'd even steal the prettiest woman in a village, a tribute to his own good looks.

What made Captain Mac most notorious
was neither his pillaging nor the means
by which he died; he was poisoned by a
jealous lover. Instead, it is Mac's funeral
for which he is most famous. It is, perhaps,
why sightings of his ghost are frequent to
this day.

Captain Mac never had a home, as he
stayed wherever he chose. Nevertheless,
he most often stayed in the town of
Belfast, Maine. It is there he was poisoned
by a nefarious woman on Friday the 13th
of October 1832.

A few days later, the entire town attended
the funeral, which began in the village
square. Captain Mac was presented in his
casket of mahogany for all to pay tribute.
It is said that by the end of the service, his

face was a solid red, covered with the lipstick of heartbroken women from Halifax to Boston.

After the ceremony, the casket was closed, and Mac was placed in the back of the funeral carriage. It was a state-of-the-art funeral carriage, complete with rollers that allowed the pallbearers to easily slide the casket in and out of the back.

The procession led from the town square to the top of the hill overlooking Belfast, a vista now known as Coffin Rock. When the carriage made it to the top, only then did the townsfolk witness the true horror. You see, the funeral director had taken ill that day, and in his place was a young apprentice, Mickey McCrady.

McCrady had never driven the funeral carriage before and didn't know how to lock the casket in place with a pin.

Upon reaching the top of the hill over-looking the town, McCrady parked his carriage with the back facing downhill. Once the villagers had circled around the open grave, McCrady opened the back of the carriage, but the weight of Captain Mac's casket was too great. The carriage doors burst open, and McCrady was no match. The grass was wet, McCrady slipped, and the casket slid down the hill.

Despite several able men chasing after it, Captain Mac was off and gone, flying over Coffin Rock, and down into Belfast. The townsfolk watched with horror as it slid through the field below, smashed through a dozen rows of corn, skipped across the frozen stream, and plummeted into the center of town. They winced, afraid to see the lid pop off and poor Captain Mac's lifeless body spill out onto the ground. But it never did. It just kept going; past the pub and grange hall, past the barrels of whiskey and stacks of lobster traps, and straight across Main Street, smashing through the front window of the pharmacy. The casket slid all the way up the aisle, just missing Old Lady Cane, and slammed into the counter, where the pharmacist was left aghast.

The lid popped open, and Captain Mac himself sat up and said, "**Got anything to stop my coffin?**"

Credits

The jokes published in this book were collected over many nights under the stars, telling stories by a campfire. A lot of them are from authors unkown, and they appear in many other collections. The rest of them can be credited to the following pirates.

Mike Callahan
Pages 33, 39, 57, 73, 89, 91

Katherine Callahan
Pages 49, 63, 67

Grace Callahan
Pages 59, 69, 71, 81

Teddy Stoecklein
Pages 9, 13, 23, 29, 37, 41, 45, 47, 51, 55, 61, 65, 75, 77, 79, 83, 87, 93, 95, 99, 101, 103, 105*

*_The Ghost of Captain Mac_ is an adaptation of a story told to me by an old friend, Greg Dickey. Greg and I worked at a cemetery together in 1991. He is one of the funniest men I've ever met.

Acknowledgments

I'd like to thank Captain Mike Callahan; his first mate Krissy, and their two deckhands, Katherine and Grace. Many of the pirate jokes you'll find here are the result of the hours we spent together roaming the islands of Maine.

I'd like to thank the hooligans at The VIA Agency who forever make life an adventure, in particular, buccaneers Duane Holmblad, for his treasure trove of really bad jokes; Lauren Rodrigue, Morgan Gelfand, Amy Waterman, Barry Wolford, Marissa Henry, and Moya Fry, for the wee hours raiding the pubs of Worcester, where many of these jokes were tested; Morgan Mitchell, who pushed me to draw dastardly things every day; Patti Lanigan, for proofreading a phonetically written book of pirate jokes, which I wrote ignoring all of Strunk & White's *Elements of Style*; John Coleman, who created a home for misfits and raconteurs alike — where creativity is currency; and my late friend Greg Smith, who found laughter in everything.

A special thanks to my mom, who opened the door to a creative life, and to my dad, who gave me the freedom to find my own voice, even if with a pirate accent.

And to my own captain, JoElle. She has provided ballast since the day we met. Here's to sails full of wind.

www.ingramcontent.com/pod-product-compliance
Lightning Source LLC
Chambersburg PA
CBHW060947040426
42445CB00011B/1047